THE BRASS GIRL BROUHAHA

T0154366

THE BRASS GIRL BROUHAHA

Adrian Blevins

AUSABLE PRESS
2003

Cover art: "Flora" (detail) by Tedd Blevins
Design and composition by Ausable Press
The type is Perpetua with Perpetua Titling.
Cover design by Rebecca Soderholm

Published by
AUSABLE PRESS
1026 HURRICANE ROAD, KEENE NY 12942
www.ausablepress.com

Distributed by
PERSEUS DISTRIBUTION SERVICES
1094 FLEX DRIVE
JACKSON, TN 38301
Toll-free: 800-283-3572
Fax: 800-351-5073

The acknowledgments appear on page 111 and constitute
a continuation of the copyrights page.

Library of Congress Cataloging-in-Publication Data
Blevins, Adrian, 1964—
The brass girl brouhaha / by Adrian Blevins.
p. cm.
ISBN 1-931337-09-8 (hardcover : alk. paper)
ISBN 1-931337-10-1 (pbk. : alk. paper)
I. Title.

PS3602.L475B73 2003
811'.6–dc21
2003013252

For my parents
and Nate

THE BRASS GIRL BROUHAHA

Life History

The Other Cold War

The Last Lap of the Daytona 500

Ritual and Rhetoric of the North American Baby Shower

Channel 58

LIFE HISTORY

For families will not be broken. Curse and expel them, send their children wandering, drown them in floods and fires, and old women will make songs out of all these sorrows and sit in the porches and sing them on mild evenings. Every sorrow suggests a thousand songs, and every song recalls a thousand sorrows, and they are infinite in number, and all the same.

—Marilynne Robinson

LIFE HISTORY

I got this nose-shaped bruise on my left arm from falling into a
      rack of dolls at Wal-Mart.
This scar on my ring finger came from when I put my hand into
      a beehive when I was two,
a calamity about which I wept into Daddy's lissome clavicle for
      three and a half months.

As for the stretchmarks, don't ask about the stretchmarks.
      There are men who like them,
but men are liars making lairs, body-shaped soul-boats of
      stretchmark-making liquids
and big ideas about the beauty of women. I've been around. I
      know what makes a woman

beautiful. This scar under my eye is from when I played mouse
      with my cat Sebastian.
I am not sure how cats could leave a mark, but with me they do.
It's as though they wish to marry me or say *hello, hello*
      perpetually.

In photographs of me as a baby, I'm white space all over.
Now in this early fall of my thirty-eighth year there are freckles,
      moles,
and other assorted blotches. They say it's sun damage, maybe
      one day will be cancer.

Let us wait and see. When you get born, you're as blue as a
        bad painting of Saturn
in the middle of the night. When you're that blue, they might
        think you didn't make it.
They might think you opted out at the last minute, climbing a
        cable of light

to some spirit world fiesta. But really you're just getting the
        slow hang of gasping.
You're signing up for the Orientation, taking notes via the
        sluggish apparatus of your lungs
while they cut off the cord and take ten names for test drives.

Then you start to breathe. Then you turn pink. The more you
        wail, the pinker you get.
It's not the pink of salmon, and it's not the pink of tongue.
It's not the pink of the sunset or the pink of Matisse's "Portrait
        of Madame Matisse"

for I-don't-know-how-much money. This pink is the pink of the
        long inhale.
I know because I saw a dead woman who was chiefly dissected,
and she was the color of sand. I looked at her and felt nothing.

I wondered if she was Eskimo. I cut my toe here walking up the
stairs.
I knocked my head against the medicine chest and thereby got
indented.
My heart sometimes jumps and skips a beat. I don't know how I
harmed it,

but I'm sure it was some blunder or another—one of the times
I took a pill, drank tequila, or gave birth against my will. Maybe
it was when I told Daddy
my crying days were over and took up gulping stones.

But let's assume for the purposes of being accurate
that it was that long ago morning I first attempted speech,
burrowing out of myself like a sulky spider, climbing the cliff of
unremitting self-infliction,

saying you—and you, and you, and you, and you—will one day
pay for this.

LIFE AND ART

This is the main story about how I hate my father. I tell you
      now in case I forget

or in case the stars plunge and he dies in an alley in Greece
or while licking the mongoose bristles of his brush
or while dipping their iota hairs into the thick yellow of an egg.

My father is not ancient or ailing, but he *will* die, since
      succumbing

is his periscope, his post office box, the bulging enterprise
      he's so famous for.
He's this way to spite me or to ebb this cantankerous singing
or because he was born doing it, as I was born inside the
      painting of a grape

while he looked on with his cigarette

and I tried not to blink and scanned the place for some way
      out—
for boats and burrows a good twelve months' wide.
Since I could write a message with it, I'll say here I caught some
      seaweed

and weave something he might hear, something like HERE!
      HERE!

since it also says: *I love you, I always have, don't forget.*
Nevertheless he with his immigrant eye keeps watching me.
He's eating peanuts, he's got the TV going, the volume's down,

there's beer in the fridge. *There's Greece in May,* my father
       would say if he could talk:

There's this brief daughter on the brink, the first ha and then the second,
the low, rolling bark she won't quit braying no matter the oceans I cross,
no matter which eye I close. It's her calling, a talent she got from her
       mother.

She's an assassin, it's her capital affliction, she won't forgive me
       anything.

THE FAMOUS MEN WHO MADE ME

While I made love in the mental hospital with a boy who had a
        fine-looking face
but might have been psychotic, my father taught his protégées
        to be risqué.

I'd stand in the hospital hall while the other hoodlums gathered
        in a zipper-line
for their liquid meds. I'd listen to my father's stories on the
        phone

and imagine Virginia's drunkest, most affluent town
expanding and contracting like an iris in a discothèque.

I was born in that place in 1964 before Mama left and
        everything fell to shit.
Before Mama left and everything fell to shit, Tennessee Williams
        insulted the whole town

by rubbing his pelvis against my father's guitar
while James Dickey and Ned Beatty and an entire citizenry of
        pot-smoking artists

came in and out of our house like insects gathering for a coup
        against the humdrum.
One or two of them would lift me off the ground so I could
        smell what being old and famous

was like. There are certain things about your life that you
        should not remember.
There are certain things a man should never tell his child.

This had to be what my grandmother knew in the late 1950's.
This is what drove her to offer my father a guitar if he'd give my
        mother back.

They stood grimace-to-grimace in the August night
until my mother—famous herself for being breathtaking and
        reckless—

came rushing out of the dogwoods and laid her tongue in
        Daddy's mouth.
For tonight at least, I do not blame my mother for marrying my
        father,

as I do not blame her for divorcing him. For tonight at least,
I could forgive anyone for anything. It's been almost thirty-six
        years

since I flopped out of Mama in my own lolly-gagging,
        impertinent way,
and I have learned what it took my mother the twelve years of
        her marriage to learn,

and that is that if my father had thought twice about what loving
    a woman can make happen,
I would not be worrying myself now

over the wise and famous men who acted as though they *wanted*
    me to tell on them—
as though I was born to record everything I heard them say or
    saw them do

as if that could help me now or them or you
as they die or migrate from place to place or settle down in
    armchairs

with their good wives beside them and their children safe inside
    the sleep
I was not myself allowed to know. Whenever I suck a man's
    cock

I think of the famous men my father raised me on. Whenever
    the man I am sucking
is about to come, I think of male accomplishment and lechery
    and loneliness

as if I'm sitting on a bar stool and all around me everyone is
    dying
from wanting to be noticed and loved and kissed and held and
    praised,

which is just wishing for wishing's own senseless sake, which is
    just wishing
for everything we think our fathers meant for us to know we
    would never get.

OF CLICHÉS AND SUPERSTITIONS

Why can't I say the psyche's a vast aperture into which any
        number of objects
might plummet or be poured? Or *soul*, the damned thing.
Because presently I'm draining *A Garden of Herbs* into that
        little hothouse

we call the psyche or the soul. Presently it's almost summer
        again
and again at noon on the Solstice I'll be a year older.
The way to know it's summer in Virginia is to watch the
        mountains

blow the spring fog out of the limestone fissures and cold trout
        dells.
Because everything *does* dissipate. Doesn't it? Presently I'm a
        big, fat liar
since actually it's still just May and I'm hot and restless in the
        city

and the back deck's got arthritis from the tonnage of the
        predictable yellow pollen
that through the window I can see I need to scrub, but would
        rather sniff and lick.
As a child I kept myself folded in like a lounge chair

and watched the at-hand extravaganza froth up on the patio,
where the hippies were always drinking too much
and bitching about the mess with the Republicans

or with the dim-witted college administration where my father
    taught art.
Darling, he would say, *This is dire, dire.* There are always
    hunters.
They come with their backpacks and zippers and tobacco pipes
    and odes.

They come with their old stones for hearts and bellies as empty
as washed-out Mayan pots. If I knew it, I'd say now the tonic.
I'd write out the recipe: borage and dried clove pounded down
    to a fine powder

and boiled in a blue glass at midnight. I read in *A Garden of*
    Herbs
that "in the southern states of America the Negroes consider it
    unlucky
to transplant parsley from one house to the next,"

so I pulled the herb I'd transplanted the day before and tossed in
      the trash.
Then I began to wash some dishes. The birds were going mad in
      the trees.
I said to them to stop clamoring me with their relentless,
      illegible clamor

when I saw the two fingers cut in four places and the sink
      flooded in my blood.

THE INTERROGATIVE SENTENCE

Do you realize nothing you say will ever make any difference
because all you do is squawk out thumps in the futile rage of
        birds?

Do you agree that birds sing syrupy in April but livid in June?

Is that because the birds' delicate, home-birthed nestlings
have moved into their own condominiums and are now sharing
        recipes for cocktails
with their excessively-sexual neighbors?

Or is it the impending snow that gets them so frantic and mad?

How do birds know about anything that's impending?

Do they also know that the sonnet has only one forefather and
        that that is the plow
and that the plow's forefather is the shift from season to season
        and from day to night
and that you should have said *foremother* just now

but did not think to do it until it was too late?

What are you supposed to think when the plows are tractors
and the tractors are air-conditioned and the air-conditioning
        chills you
even when it's one hundred degrees outside and all the plants
        are flaccid?

Do you realize your Ex and not-Ex husbands are completely
        unalike
and therefore can't stand one another

but are unable to admit it, being Neanderthals who prefer
        silence to hurtful talking?

What kind of talking is not hurtful?

Do you think the husbands are probably right?

Do you think you're a tyrant?

Do you think you're stuck in your own bed of words and that
        the world could explode
for all you could care
        as long as you had some literature with you

as long as you had not written it yourself?

Is that why you're so tired?

Is it true that you love nothing more than your children, except
    writing?

Is it true that you neglect your children for writing the way
    your father did you
when he'd paint and you'd squawk

and nothing you ever said made any difference

because that's the way he was and you got his syndrome

which is the syndrome of the uncorrectable sorrow
that enters the painter's eyes and the poet's mouth?

Are you the bird you know you are and is rage your middle
    name?

WOMEN'S LIB

You were born half out of your mind in love with your mother.
Not crazy, but ditzy and bemused, your hot-pink tot-tongue

sucking the edge of a yellow blanket.

That's because you were made on purpose to animate her
        house—
the one she lived to buff and polish. Your mother was good at
        houses;

houses could be said to be her calling; she couldn't stomach

the dust or ashes—the paint chips, red and black and gold—
that fell off your father like rain. You'd watch him at his easel;

he'd lick his brush before he'd paint the model-girl's pubic hair.

Meanwhile she'd strip an antique and categorize his books;
meanwhile she'd place twelve shimmering crystal glasses atop a
        crystal plate.

He was as spellbound as you were, he could hardly speak;

she was a whirlwind and crooning yellow chime,
choking death and trouble with a nightly fire and good rope
        mop.

16

And then, as though it wouldn't confound the pretty birds

warbling in the maples and the oaks
and cast a wicked shade on the faces of the TV mammals

and defile your bread with cinders and set the beds to jarring,

she was standing in the back yard with a cigarette in her mouth
burning his painting of a girl

who looked for all the world like a tongue-tied Christmas angel.

She was singing something by Aretha Franklin.
She was saying enough was enough.

He was somewhere else. He was painting, singing, grieving,

weeping; he was standing in a meadow reciting Wallace Stevens.
He was pulling out his hair or sleeping in a parking lot

or purring into the neck of someone named Amy

while you sat in the sunlight
and laced and unlaced your mint-condition tennis shoes.

OUR LADY OF PERPETUAL BAD LUCK

The good brides of Christ are not children and they are not
    men.

Since they aren't women either, I've got to say they're saints.
Right now, middle-aged, they fill Our Lady of Perpetual Bad
    Luck
with songs about Jesus in high, festive notes.

Oh, I'm nothing like a nun—I'm a nun's worst nightmare—
I've got three children out there getting arrested, feeling low,
saying *Mama, Mama, where did Mama go?*

If I could move, I'd call them.

Instead I eavesdrop on the nuns long past dinnertime
and remember where my own mother split apart between her
    legs—
that smell she made like the woods at night on moldy fire.

She's standing at the sink, white suds are stockpiled like
    electrified spit
all around her, and my Daddy's prattling, as usual.

She smells him smell her, too, I know it drives my panic,
I watch my heart twist to lemon slices.

So, then: he's pouring a drink, he's rubbing her back.

He's saying, *Let's go to D.C., let's take a little trip, let's have another*
   baby, let's go upstairs right now.

But she's saying, *It's dinnertime,* she's looking out the window,
she's already got the boyfriend.

Or let's say she's leaning against a wall, wearing a party dress.
Let's say my father's already banished and she's laughing up a
   storm
at something the boyfriend's just said or his guitar or just him
   himself.

The *marvel* of him, that's what she's pining to convey—
the way the water gushes at the river where they eat their secret
   picnics
is perhaps the metaphor.

She's clearly full of delusions, my mother in fervent love,
and thus so high on him I feel the need to scream.

Yet I've got to be fair this instant and say—nuns are *virgins*—
how I packed away my pouty face and joined her fiendish tribe,
   Oh, anyway.

GENERALLY SPEAKING

All the notable things that ever happened to me happened out of
    love.
My mother, Titian blonde and thin and a woman with so many
    words in her mouth
it's a wonder they didn't fall out of her in a twelve-point font

while she stood at the stove over sweet-and-sour chicken,

left me one night. The shadow in her wake was so immense,
    such a bald-faced prologue,
it fell all the way into the nineties like a fashion I saw coming,
    but couldn't predict.
She'd fallen in love, that's the thing, with a man who made
    objects out of wood.

But all the time before that my father had been slinking out of
    bed

to meet some student or another at the motel down the road, so
    I can't blame her.
I'd like to talk to those girls now, to ask them what they thought
    they were doing
with my father. I'd like to buy them a drink, invite them in my
    house

to look me straight in the eye and then I'd serve them—

I'd serve them champagne and a very chocolate cake.
Look, it was the early seventies and I don't blame anyone for
    having a heart.
If I'd been my mother, I would have fallen in love with the
    wooden man.

I would have gone anywhere with him—would have ridden a
    horse

to every hallowed land. And if I'd been one of my father's
    students,
I would have wanted him out of his house, and I would not have
    considered
his wife there, or his daughters, or anything at all

but that he might love me enough to die for. And this is what it
    always

comes down to, no matter the decade, no matter whose body:
wanting to be buried alive in whatever we didn't get when we
    needed it most,
with what wasn't there when we were eleven and sat in flannel
    on the staircase

with our hands under our chins. We were there, we were
     breathing,

and devoured even then the high-blown mutiny perfume
(like the scent of hope screaming to be let out)
of someone blowing in the alley on a good, brass trumpet.

THE OTHER COLD WAR

❦

"Being a together woman is a bitch," say Marcy.
"Being a bitch is a bitch," say Gail.
"Men a bitch," is my two cents...

—*Toni Cade Bambara*

THE OTHER COLD WAR

I am the girl who knows better but. ——John Berryman

If you want to know what my lousy childhood was like
and how my parents were occupied and all before they had me

and all that [defunct, whiney, Anne Sexton] *kind of crap,*
I don't mind, I'm not shy, I'll tell you. But first let me say

I was born as mute as a white Dixie cup in a cattle-pissing
        stream
with just my eyes for talking, with just my cotton pout of a
        mouth.

But then something snapped and I'm not saying the vocal
        chords.
I'm not saying worries in the rain like *does he love me, does he not.*

I'm talking a much more foremost evil ambition—
talking the sway that spawned in my crotch

and rose through my belly and climbed up my throat
to shape the vowels that to the boys said *yes.*

I'm talking the feigned plea of the blink and put-on lick of the
        kiss
that would trigger the kick of bowling them over.

I'm talking the chief assault of the pubescent trot,
the poor moon through the window, the bites on my lip.

I'm talking the violence and the violation of the say-so and the
      clout
since it got me their anguish once I said we were over—

that rancid begging of *please, more trouble*—
that reduction of them to nothing but rubble.

FAILING THE REPUBLIC

Back when I was fifteen faking older and working at Pizza Hut
for two-dollars-an-hour plus tips, taking an order was like
      Sartre in German

and the whole history of the horrible world in sand-sketched
      hieroglyphics
though all I had to do was write a *P* for Pan or a *T* for Thin.

All I had to do was mark the squares designating toppings—
did the people want green peppers, onions, mushrooms, bacon?

But the multitudes standing at the door
couldn't wait to tap the tables for Coke and beer and salad
      bowls.

Did the people want me to say how good they looked in their
      hair?
Did they want me to lick their gaping places?

All I had was quarters for the jukebox and an inkling that I was a
      calamity.
All there *was* was the phone that wouldn't stop ringing

since the people were after Take Out since their babies were
      hungry
and their husbands missing or in high-rise apartments in distant
      Chicago.

Hunger in this two-faced train town
was always an opus of woe wadding my head with the needs of
      the people

until what could I do but pronounce them all asses
and walk out the door? I could have taken a taxi or called my
      mom,

but it was far more dramatic to run down Hershberger
and turn on to Peters Creek

and keep on going past the 7-Eleven and the whole city heaving
until I came to the hungry and sulky-hearted populace of the
      graveyard.

Good riddance, haughty, baffled girl, the unappeasables must've
      thought.
Good riddance, unappeasables, I the imposter-waitress of the
      insatiable ire

(these twenty-five years later) bark back.

THE MAGNIFICENCE OF RAIN

Since I thought you had to be self-murderous or homosexual if
    you had literary aspirations

and since ambition was the main venom in my young-person
    heart
and I was as smiling-obliging as a salesman in Atlanta
if I was after something I thought I wanted,

I tried one day to be a lesbian.

The point of sex during that era was to trick men out of their
    indifference
and make them love me within twenty-four hours.
The point of sex during that era was to make men bow down to
    the princess I thought I was

and moreover abandon their mothers and moreover their
    automobiles.

I wanted men to beg me to take them back
even if I had not abandoned them yet. I wanted them to take
    me for a wife
so I could decorate their cabins with myself in the kitchen
    baking bread

or myself nude on the couch with my hair as fierce as slaughter.

Thus my woman-lover's tongue did nothing for me. The
women on this earth?
We are all befuddled. Even that one so long ago—that trial
lover with the petite hands
who said I was too magnificent for men. She was *quite*

mistaken. I am just a cold body wailing my rain all over this
world.

GIRL, EIGHTH GRADE, TWO OR THREE COPIES OF *THE AUTOBIOGRAPHY OF MALCOM X* LYING AROUND THE HOUSE

Once she no longer appears to have been appealing,
after her face is a full-fade and a gone-gray wiper-blade,
she will stop wondering why she didn't stop that unknown boy

from fingering her in the theatre. This was '76 or '77,
and the movement or the cause or whatever you want to call it
was still hot soup in her parents' hearts.

Maybe there were BLACK POWER! bumper stickers
on her Barbie's Corvette. In the cinema all she could see of the
          boy
were the whites of his eyes. Isn't it funny, being a child?

She thought she was being *polite*.
She thought she would hurt the boy's feelings
if she asked him to take his finger out,

or his *Mama's* feelings, and hadn't *her* Mama's Mama
been born a slave and wasn't that appalling
and shouldn't this sin be avenged

by white girls like her with long blonde hair and blue blue eyes?
Who cares if the white kids called her a nigger lover in school
and licked their teeth with their country tongues

when she walked in the cafeteria to eat the fake pizza
they served on Fridays? And who cares if she figured the strange
        boy
had already taken her virginity with his finger

and so lost it for real two months later with a white boy
in a Mustang? The thing is that she barely remembers this.
For all she knows she kissed him too

and rubbed his nappy head against her nothing chest
and came there in the dark, trembling vastly and deciding thusly
to YES and YES and YES and *YES*.

The thing is that this is not a political poem
about American race relations, but an unembellished ode
to one girl's idyllic undoing.

DEFECTS OF THE ADOLESCENT

Didn't she after all put herself out there like an hors d'oeuvre
        on a pewter platter?
And didn't boys after all appear and hand over their smokes?

The boys would stand there with their lips trembling
until she was magically in the garden extending her wrist and
        pinching off a rose stem.

And maybe one would put something in her hair.
And maybe he'd cry and slump to his knees and commence his
        pathetic begging.

And maybe she'd smile, but probably she'd just turn her back
and rouse in her mind the pros and cons of fucking him:

he'd be grateful, he'd be proud, it wouldn't be worth a god-
        damned shit,
it would take him three seconds. Therefore at twenty-two

she married a spiritual man. He would close his eyes and listen
        to Rilke
and weep over Rilke and quote Rilke and Yeats and especially
        Faulkner.

And besides the clichéd eastern ideas
that seem to come with being American and young,

they were all right for a long while, living without bodies.
They spawned sons as sociologists spawn inexplicable prose:

they did it to obfuscate their friends in the humanities
or for the sake of home birth or so they could use cloth diapers

and openly condemn Proctor and Gamble for filling up the
        landfills.
They did it so she could nurse her babies in the shopping mall

and thereby reveal the naked breast she felt she had to expose
because what it did was signify

all the hope and misery she could muster.
All she could think was that if she laid out the merchandise,

the good men and women with their bodies still intact
would come around to occupy her rocking chairs

and want her homemade honey pies
that for all their time and money and blood and love

she would maybe—and maybe not—relinquish.

MID-DIVORCE WEATHER REPORT

Last night I tried to say some things
about the things that don't or can't get said.

Maybe that's why this morning's hollandaise curdled up
like it thought I was foolish and had to knit its brow.

Since I didn't know why not,
I ate it over eggs and bacon.

Before you and I put on our knapsacks,
what did we speak of? In that final moment,

why couldn't I close my eyes
and put my fingers to your mouth?

Why couldn't we say what would become of us
once our marriage hung the CLOSED sign

in its unreasonable yellow window?
I don't know what you'll think of me

after I am dead. I mean, I know so little
now. For instance: why can't you hear those insects

just outside the kitchen door?
They sound to me like children telling lies.

One day soon, I'll give my sorrow up.
I'll tell our boys fate's a slow star

spinning toward them from the sun.
I'll tell them they've got this life and not one other.

But already the sky's too ardent
in their little sundial faces. *Mom,* they say,

we've lost our goddamned hats. Hey Mom,
they say, *we think it's going to rain.*

TURNING THIRTY-SIX

I've never told the story of my mourning body. It's not much of
    a story.
It's a sickbed story made of graveyard refuse.
I achieved my mourning body with sorrow and starvation and
    blotch.

I rejected water, I cast off wine,
I sat among weeds below brown finches crooning and said
    deplete, deplete,
deplete. I loved my mourning body so immeasurably

I'd lie vigilant in bed and trace the blade of each protruding
    bone,
remembering the husband who'd left and the mother who'd left
and their psycho-goblins in the psycho air.

Or maybe I'd remember the unholy remains of a spectral mare
some turn-of-the-century farmer had tossed in a shallow creek
between the evergreen ridges of my grandmother's tree farm.

My sister and I would stand there, staring at the pelvis
or the skull, touching or licking the bleached shoulder blades.
We knew nothing, then. We were just children, then.

Oh, we knew death was out there, flying overhead like a yellow
      canary
while bellowing in the trees like a brass trombone,
but what could we have known of the births that would take our
      bodies from us?

No matter what, the bodies of girls will fatten on semen and
      burgeon with milk
while the fathers with zilch in their hands amble off drunk,
      broke, bawling, blind.
In their divergent dreams do the febrile men see us as we once
      were,

when we were still little birds in the water? Do they carry us in
      the pockets
of their hearts? Do they take us out and throw us down
while we rock like hags in the deadbeat dark?

SPY STORY

Sometimes I shrink to the size of a yellowjacket and fly into a
        fissure
and hang my tiny eye from the ceiling in his kitchen.

There I watch him pout or prick his finger.

Sometimes he sits on the floor and does a little math;
sometimes he makes orange juice

or stares into the photos of our two children
or picks up some stained glass

and smashes it against his thigh.

Sometimes he sings some old folk song or calls me and gets no
        answer;
sometimes he writes a letter about every evil thing I ever said or
        did to him,

making a great comic collage out of our marriage,
getting out the magazines and the glue—
cutting out the eye of a bobcat and the leg of a fox,
scissoring the word NOSE from four different fonts,

then splashing water on his face to try and quench the fuming
        rant
on why he's right to hate me.

Poor him, working along at nothing while I hid out in my study
and brushed and unbrushed my hair.

Poor me, watching him jump on the DC subway train when we
      were still eighteen
and crying on the midnight platform
until he came back to say

he'd marry me and save me
and plant an orchard nowhere near the sea.

Later he would bury two of my placentas, saying prayers over
      them.
Later I'd kick him out and wish him dead for doing what I
      wanted—

for packing up his cameras and his sandals
and heading to his forest house

with the owls and raccoons
hunched like beggars in the bushes.
There the next girl was, waiting with her hair in a blue
      bandanna.

Then, this past July, came their tiny child,
each of her five pounds propped like atomic stones
against my so-called heart.

HANSEL ON THE HIGHROAD

Even before I knew all the will you've got to lose to love a man
I would pretend to sleep in my grandmother's house

and think of Hansel. I wanted Hansel's haphazard wandering,
his pilfered birdseed, his blood. I wanted to love him right then
    and there.

I wanted to love him in the woods and trees
and on the eaves of that roof made of sugar.

And even if it *was* Gretel who murdered the witch gone mad
of loneliness and longing, it was Hansel who gave her the
    muscle.

It was Hansel, in time, who'd assault the tide with his
    indignation.
It was Hansel, Hansel, *Hansel* I wanted.

It was Hansel who so understood misery I dreamed he'd bless
    me with it
and make me quake in bed—Hansel who'd sink into me, Hansel
    who'd stay there.

So when the forest would darken and the wild eyes of the
    treacherous animals
would blink awake, Hansel, keeping watch, would just stare
    back at them.

He would dare them, under God, to enter.
He would bide, under God, his time.

He would sing for the sake of the tussle itself this song of the
    always-wounded
and in my grandmother's bed I would swallow the praise that
    came from his throat

and lick a string of spit around my finger
and writhe around in that line-dried, sheet-boat of sweat.

I would open and close my empty fist and for Hansel forgive all
    our fathers
their crimes against us and for Hansel thank God for Hansel.

Hansel, I mean, in the daybreak. Hansel howling out my name
from the missing rib vowel by vowel into vow.

It is *Hansel* I sing for. He'll know me. He'll listen. He'll come.

THE LAST LAP OF THE DAYTONA 500

My mother says, This one will never be satisfied with anything. I think I'm beginning to see my life. I think I can already say, I have a vague desire to die. From now on I treat that word and my life as inseparable. I think I have a vague desire to be alone, just as I realize I've never been alone any more since I left childhood behind, and the family of the hunter. I'm going to write.

—*Marguerite Duras*

UNUSUAL SUMMER WEATHER

This overstated thunderstorm is a fancy blue hat
upon the very brink of which Zeus is perched and crooning,
poking out his godly pinkie while sipping good Zinfandel

and catapulting seedless grapes down into the Nile
or into the hot and steamy redwood tubs on the weather-
        proofed decks
of the women of the DC start-ups. That is,

he's crashing roller coasters and hitting small children
upon their anemic heads and pulling out his loincloth pennies,
licking them for luck. He listens all day

for the plunk and holler of the children on their slides
and chain-link swings and plastic motorbikes.
That's when the Moms come running with their bras half-
        snapped

and their panties askance. Whereupon Zeus rubs his belly
with olive oil and powder puffs his golden hair
and bids the Orchestra pluck *Sweet Home Alabama*

and knots tiny rose blooms into the straps of his sandals
and giggles over at Venus lying on a towel
under a colossal brass lamp, sunning her glossy skin

like a lizard on a rock
while down below we bitch and moan and whine and weep
like demons, like puppies, like newborns in our beds.

XANTHE, THE MASTER GARDNER, DIES AT 50 OF AN UNHAPPY MARRIAGE

If I have a bird's nest in my heart, it is not made of lemon leaves,
since I have never seen a lemon tree as such flora won't grow
    here

and I have never been anywhere else. To imply that lemon trees
grew in this piece of Virginia would perjure me

before the esteemed clubs and alliances of the malcontented
    homebodies
who have certificates of Garden Knowledge in heaven.

My friend Xanthe for example died in January when everything
    was latent
because what she hated, besides her husband with his pitiless
    theories

about everyone opting for whatever they got, was the winter.
More rightly, what Xanthe hated was herself for not knowing
    twenty years ago

how she'd come to feel about her husband the week before she
    decided
she'd rather die than look at him an extra second, since being
    young was obsolete

and anyway impossible, like the quilt her mother never gave her,
which matched exactly in shape and color the antique locket

her father also never gave her, since he just walked out one day
and never came back. If I have a bird's nest in my heart, it is not
    even made

of wisteria vine, though we planted wisteria out back against the
    fence,
wanting, in other words, a sombrero, a little bougainvillea, a
    vacation in California—

oh, please just give me and my baby some endless days of heat
and by this means some west coast plants so we can buy an
    encyclopedia

that names for a living the names of trees not-cypress, not-
    scrub-pine,
not-spruce. Or Xanthe! Xanthe would say my bird's nest heart

is not made of bottle caps or lost Emu hair or the torn-off scraps
of failed compositions. Xanthe would ridicule the whole bird's
    nest metaphor

entirely. She'd tell me my heart was a muscle of buoyant bloody
    cells,
then blow the spent leaf of a local plant far-off and away.

STORY OF THE WISCONSIN BLIZZARD

A young mother driving her son through a Wisconsin blizzard
in a wool dress imprinted to echo a winter garden. Between
　　　her breasts

hangs a silver pendant of one religious-seeming swan.
It dangles from the fat leather lace her little sister Alice,

that morning in the yellow kitchen, pulled, grinning, from an
　　　orphan shoe.
The mother bought the pendant because the swan's eyes seemed
　　　to her ascended,

and why not because he missed his long-lost cousin, the sun?
There's another motor—a grand thing, a fatal hitch—coming
　　　toward them

like a faint, and the tiny boy in his red coat and palm-sized
　　　Christmas boots
practicing his alphabet or saying how Billy had a grandfather, an
　　　uncle,

and a dad, so why couldn't he? Otherwise just this January
　　　silence
like the deepest water under water. She pulls into what might
　　　or might not

be the ditch; she lengthens her neck to listen. The plow cuts off
        the top
of her Volkswagen, taking her head with it. And so her body
        sags

over the boy, knocking him to the floorboard. All night she
        mothers him:
all that lessening heat. Then the college students with their long
        arms

and forest-colored coats come and touch his face. He grows in
        good time
in his grandmother's house and forgets the story of the
        Wisconsin blizzard

except for sometimes, like for instance when women leave him
and there's this trace of them left in the room or bar or bed—

the lingering scent of Rachel's just-washed hair, for instance:
Wheat Germ and Jojoba is what he'd read on the bottle. Story
        after story,

terror after terror. Cancer, car wrecks, the Asian bird virus, the
        busted heart,
the chilled limb—everything as if quite on purpose blown
        wholly apart.

January; unreasonably benign weather; lots and lots of rain.
I pick up seven squirming earthworms and put them in a jelly
    jar.

There they are on the windowsill, stilling in the eerie sun one
    by one by one.

THE LAST LAP OF THE DAYTONA 500

When Dale Earnhardt dies, I'm standing in Uncle Doc's
      kitchen,
listening to the men put across the woe of the penalty of
      NASCAR.
Since this is the day of Ann's funeral and most of us have driven
      a long way
to hear the Episcopalians in their smart white robes say all but
      nothing
about Ann who lived among us our entire lives as we ourselves
      lived among us
since she was also us, it seems to the men unfeasible that beyond
      Ann's death
there's now the death of Dale Earnhardt, Dale Earnhardt,
      Dale Earnhardt.

Before the wreck (get this) I was writhing as only I would
that the men were watching the race while the women prepared
      some casseroles.
Unlike Ann, I was writhing. Then the knock and the spin and
      the splash
of the crash, and even if the men didn't drop their glasses and
      fall to their knees
and weep, you could tell that's what they were after with all
      their hollering.
Knowing that made me think that the empty winter trees
      looked like nerve endings
as we drove from Ann's casket and the immaculate church there
      below

the sun. The winter trees know there's no sense in trying to
    change people.
O uncles, cousins, fathers, brothers: sit in your chairs all week
    long
and mourn the death of the great stock car racer Dale
    Earnhardt, if you want.
This poem reviles instead the rubbish Episcopalians speak in
    small Virginia chapels
re: my mother's sister Ann who died of a hard-working,
    charitable heart
while downstairs in the dark Earnhardt blazed in churning
    spheres of counterfeit light.

BILLY JOEL GETS PHILOSOPHICAL ON BRAVO

That thing Billy said about how we enter someone's heart when
    we die?

It's not *A Brief History of Time* or anything, but what if Billy's
    right?

What if the heart really is a doorway with a silver lock and
    dying, that's the key?

Let's say you die and live in a little apartment in someone's
    heart.

Let's say you've got a red velvet chair, an old floor lamp,
    and a library filled with all the books you didn't get to
    read alive.

Let's say there's a cute little deli down the road
    and a radio that plays all your favorite songs from the
    sixties and seventies
    and also, on Sunday afternoons, the folk songs, the Knees
    Deep in Big Muddy.

There'd also be tea bags and after dinner mints.

There'd be a mammoth pile of handwritten letters from
      everyone who ever hurt you,
        sealed at the point of envelope entry with the person's
           initials in wax,
      and the prose—the prose would be outstanding—

it would include that loneliness of horses line
      from James Wright's *if I could step out of my body* poem
      and descriptions of everything Hieronymous Bosch
      ever thought he shouldn't, but couldn't help but think.

The weird thing would be when someone *else* died
      and entered this heart that was your apartment and
        library and deli.

What if he or she didn't like your radio?

What if he or she turned off your floor lamp and sat in the dark
      despondent about the lack of drugs in this, the Piano
        Man hereafter?

I'm finding it difficult to live with people. Even the people I
love.

As for strangers: you may as well know that's asking a bit too
		much—
	that's like knocking on my door and wanting me to
		believe in angels.

When the housekeeping women in their delicate, prairie-girl
		clothing
	show up with their bibles and small-print documents on
		the splendor of heaven,
	I say I'm sorry, but I'm quite the homosexual.

My sister, on the other hand, once hid in her closet.

What was it like in there? Was there a single light bulb
		hanging from a white socket in the ceiling?

Did she stare at all the coats or rummage through the pockets
		of the rejected toddler trousers
		while the women knocked and hollered *yoo-hoo*
		in their high-wire voices?

Is that what being dead is? Hiding in the dark with out-of-style
		outerwear?

What kind of person would stay up all night
		thinking about the philosophy of Billy Joel?

Do you know?

Would you please just *tell me* before the angels materialize
in their onionskin caps and black taxicabs?

KINGS OF THE TRAMPOLINE

The story of the woman who'd been shot in her neck in the
        Texaco
got straight away complicated by the story of how I was
        hearing it

with a baby on my hip. Then the story of how she bled to death

on the very spot I happened to be standing
with a pack of cigarettes and a tiny cherry sucker the color of a
        nipple

got complicated by the picture-book story of the pig Olivia

from *Olivia Saves the Circus,* since the baby and I went right home
and read it. Olivia paints Jackson Pollocks on the living room
        wall

and lies about being Queen of the Trampoline to her teacher,

who you can tell from the frowning expression on his pig-
        teacher face
is annoyed with Olivia for just being Olivia. Yet the obvious
        point of the book is,

isn't Olivia cute? Olivia's cute, all right; Olivia and her
        shenanigans

are worth at least these breezy charcoal drawings if not a major
      motion picture.
But how much are you willing to bet the boys who shot that girl
      in the Texaco

were much like the precocious pig Olivia

with their high spirits spreading thick across their childhoods
      like pokeweed?
Can I say that all murderers are constructed out of Popsicles and
      fabric softener

and bittersweet memories about how their yellow blankets
      frayed to pieces

in their mothers' washing machines before their thumbs and
      mouths were ready?
And what about the story about how I am going to get the hell
      out of this city anyway

and buy a new place way out in the country somewhere

and also a couple of cows and also more dogs than possible?
Will my sons be less angry then? Will my picturesque sons

stop being statistics in Washington about the effect of failed
      marriages

on the child psyche, then? Will they become wholesome
      farmboys
kissing me in the kitchen in their overalls or even jumping up
      and down

on the trampoline I'll somehow get the money to buy?

Isn't *that* the story it's high time for me to tell?
And how does it begin? And how, moreover, end?

HE SAYS, SHE SAYS

Let me just say that the only thing worse
than your young husband chasing you around with a perpetual
      hard-on
while suggesting via a number of sophisticated rhetorical moves

that a lack of constant, mind-blowing sex will cause,
in addition to the Yankee insolence, a swelling of the wrists and
      ankles
and diphtheria and gangrene and maybe even *menstruation*—

maybe even the growing on of maybe even an actual *vagina*—
is your young husband, tired of your pigheaded apprehension
born of your fifty-two students and hell-bent offspring

smoking pot and failing math and wrecking cars
and necessitating thus the parent/teacher conferences
and appointments with love-thy-neighbor intervention
      specialists

and police officers and counselors
as well as the heart attack you feel you've got coming and no
      doubt deserve
as well as the leukemia that might follow it and/or your
      potential murder

and the associated little problem of where to bury you
and what to say at the funeral and where the children will live
      after that
and where they'll attend college and who'll pay for it

as well as the book—the goddamned, mother-fucking, fucking,
      fucking *book*—
is him *not* chasing you, slacking off as he is on the couch over
      there
thinking up slicked-up girls in French Maid dresses

unhooking their halters and pornographic panty snaps
and commencing thus to save him, is all he's meaning to intend,
from a perfectly-avoidable and therefore unbearably tragic
      demise.

NOVEMBER NEUROSIS

I am scared of varying my routine by even five minutes
because I'm scared of anything unsteady

because I'm scared of my children dying.

Car wrecks mostly, but burnings and drownings
and meningitis and leukemia and gunshots and bombings, as
       well.

That's how reckless the world is: it doesn't care to keep my
       children whole.

I was a giant moth in my white nursing gown
fluttering over my babies in their cribs.

I was a ghost, milky white—I'd lean down

and kiss their fleecy heads until they woke affronted.
Still I couldn't abide the dark room.

Still I *could not abide* that a man could ladder up and enter the
       unlockable room.

I'd put my babies in bed beside me then
and place my hand upon them to be sure they had heartbeats
       and pulses.

After some time my arm would throb and ache, but I would
        never move it.

The assorted husbands had to roll over or sleep on the floor
or Mastercard a King-sized bed! The assorted husbands

were immaterial unless they knew CPR.

Don't talk to me about sex, I'd say.
I'm checking her heart, I'm keeping him alive, I'm busy, don't
        talk.

I knew a girl whose brother killed her.

First he stabbed her, then he poured gasoline over her,
then he set her on fire.

In class not six months earlier

my students and I had admired the erotic energy of the girl's
        poem.
In class (not six months earlier)

the girl had put her eyes down and said, *but it's for my brother.*

He's in prison somewhere watching TV,
washing clothes, eating meat loaf.

I've thought of visiting. I've thought of saying: *Look, my babies*
  are good—

they'll do the world good, they're creative,
they pet stray dogs, they sing.

But so did his sister. She's buried, is all I'm saying.

She's lying solitary in a casket
like a black cricket under an empty counter.

She was *a child,* is all I'm saying.

The firemen found her and put her in a body bag.
I am forever worried and she is dead;

we are each of us born so holy and everlastingly molested.

RITUAL AND RHETORIC OF THE NORTH AMERICAN BABY SHOWER

You have to live in a town.
You have to live in a house.
You have to send your kids to schools.
You don't live on an airplane, drunk on miniature bottles
      of scotch,
flying coast to coast.

—*Stephanie Brown*

RITUAL AND RHETORIC OF THE NORTH AMERICAN BABY SHOWER

The women are gathering in Boston and Memphis and Tulsa and
    so on.
Even in the atmospheric condition of noxious waste below the
    pristine mountains

where I live, the women are pulling into driveways
and stepping from their minivans, holding by loosely-braided
    purple strings

sugar-dusted gift bags within which there are tiny white socks
    and diapers,
yellow ducks and Vaseline. They sit around in perfumed circles
    and commiserate.

One woman will say she just wanted her drugs.
In the old days they used The Twilight Sleep and what you did

was sink into a breathless abyss and wake up doubled if you
    were lucky
and tripled if you were not. But now they use an epidural.

One young mother will tell how the good man came in and laid
    her on her side.
She'll tell of how he injected something arctic into the fluid of
    her spine.

She'll sigh and say how she fought the urge to call people on the
        phone.
I'm having a baby! she'll admit she wanted to tell at least the
        operator,

and I can't feel a thing! What the woman won't admit
while she sits in her chair and eats her stuffed mushrooms

and eyes the expectant woman who's suddenly weeping in her
polka-dotted peasant dress despite the hundreds of sheets of
        thin white wrapping tissue

floating all around her like anemic clouds, is that she wanted to
        sleep
with the anesthesiologist. The woman remembers even now

wishing to pull that anesthesiologist's Johnboy face to her face.
She remembers wanting to run off with him to Florida or Cuba
        or even West Virginia.

Her husband may have tried then to place an ice cube in her
        mouth.
He may have sighed his slobbery sigh and fallen back into his
        useless sleep.

Nevertheless the woman went right on with her dream of
        marrying the anesthesiologist,
whom she understood she loved as trees love small, outsider-
        boys

with marbles in their pockets or as I love my own children
who are as immense and difficult as skyscrapers bending in the
        ruinous wind.

Yet the woman knew even then that the anesthesiologist could
        not save her
from this absurd condition for which there was no escape,

even when the women were all around *her* in the shower-circle
giving her soft things in pastel colors and telling their horrible
        stories

as though they were not horrible, but glorious tales of knights
        and maidens
in white dresses—oh, if she was only having the
        anesthesiologist's baby

or just swimming in some less bloody sea!
Once the women cease their damp oozing over the pregnant
        woman's fears

or the tenth sky-white, hand-sized sailor suit, I'll begin my own
      customary spewing.
And though I'll try not to shout or stand behind the podium I'll
      make with a chair,

I'll nevertheless let loose my ridiculous lecture on the virtues of
      home birth
while the women sign and twitch. There is to consider the
      violence of the episiotomy,

I'll say. There is the way in which such a thing is a violation of
      the vagina.
There's to consider the usefulness of water and walking

and the spirituality of the midwife, who could put a glove on
      her hand
and check for dilation and remind you for no good reason of
      your own good mother,

who would in fact be standing beside you going pale,
in which case childbirth could become a kind of revenge,

which is what it is if you play your cards right: her standing by
      your bed
thinking she'd better call 911 or the funeral home, the darkness
      everywhere

like the nights you stood in your crib and no one came, the
      scream you could not
quit screaming, the nameless baby's bloody head, halfway in,
      halfway out.

CHILDBIRTH

Some women are too wise,
and curse before they weep.
My grandmother did,
and look where it got her:
as dead as anything dead
one alluring April day
while inside our yearling cat
a single cell split and divided
and puffed and pumped
until this morning there's a pint of blood
sprawled across the laundry basket
like an abstract painting,
and my daughter, insane with glee,
saying we'd ourselves divided,
and the kitten, blind,
and its mother, sputtering.

She picked up the kitten by its neck
like she'd rather *eat* than nurse it,
then looked at us over her shoulder
as though it were
the most absurd thing—
all she'd gone though:
the blood she'd lost,
the vitamins she'd need
to replenish, and oh this hunger

like an empty bucket inside her belly.
And to have to lie there in the dresser
and let the baby suckle
and munch. Really, it was *degrading,*
if you wanted to know
what *she*—the Siamese—thought.

It was passé, it wasn't worth the work,
it took the steam right out of you.
They come out bawling
and incompetent; they grow huge.
They bellyache for a vocation;
they fail to learn to sing.
They'll be mothers, too,
one sunny day, and then
they'll be *grand*mothers.
Just you wait: the women
will curse you on their deathbeds,
they'll try to take it back,
and then as though to spite you—
you'll see—they'll leave.

STILL LIFE WITH PEEVED MADONNA

It's clear I'm standing on the Isle of Motherdom
given these three children hanging off my arms and feet

weighing the weight of the planet, at least.
The children look like dime-store bric-a-brac

since all that swings will squarely star-sparkle,
but more like missiles in size and expulsion intent.

They're asking how cold is the water, to which I say I don't
      know.
They're asking could they have some macaroni & cheese

to which I say I'm occupied hating this line, hush, now hush.
They're asking how far is it inland & do the natives dance there

& can they go & get some confetti & snort or inject it
to which I say years ago I could answer your questions

but look at those clouds, I think that's a cyclone
to which they say, fuck you, Mom, you're always so paranoid

to which I say, fuck you, too, you remind me of lizards,
were you birthed in an outhouse by an ogre or a loon?

THE X GAMES

When Benjamin comes in and stands in the doorway

with his hands in his pockets, I think: *He's eleven years old
and unquestionably maladjusted.* I say: *You're so beautiful,*

you should be in Hollywood and kiss him, kiss him,

kiss him. Ben is in fact quite good looking, despite
the six or seven thrasher boys screaming and stomping

inside his blood, wearing neck charms that look like dog collars.
Yet isn't it really just *Ben* standing there? He of the two

who without any papers snuck inside me during the 1980's

when all I wanted was out of my marriage or retarded
or departed? That's how angry I was, I don't mind saying:

that's how bad the sex was. For now Ben would just like to say

that Someone Someone broke his neck trying a backwards
        double flip
on his bike. I've seen it before: the boys coming out all hot and
        excessive

like they were born in Wheeling, West Virginia on a bankrupt
        carnival

ride. When I tell Ben I'm writing this poem and need to know
the name of the boy who died on his bike, he just looks at me
slow

and skateboards grinning down to Greenland Street.

I just stand there then, and let him go.

MY HAPPINESS

What I am is swept away from time to time by happiness,
which appeared without precedence one morning
like a woman from a sixth dimension nation state
walking easy-going to me in a dress made of something
as down-to-earth as trumpet vines. Sure I know
the angry boys are sucking on bullets in a hotel or hut,
thrashing out brimstone ambitions with switchblade minds,
but my happiness doesn't care, my happiness isn't political,
my happiness is made of a watery light the color of Mexican sky.

Once I believed you could avert the anger of the angry boys
by saying how Peter Rabbit almost drowned in a watering can.
But the angry boys say *fuck that* for a living
even when they'd rather repent. This I know because my own
          two angry boys
have learned the art of the grimace-face and the huff and puff of
          rage
despite my storybook intentions, wearing their bandanas for
          emphasis
and sharpening the spikes they wear on their wrists.

Sure I know I could have nursed them longer and rocked them
          softer
or taken them on field trips across the Himalayas
or had them under better circumstances and thus prevented the
          poverty

and therefore my depression and the absentminded attention
and therefore my shame. Nonetheless at the oddest moments
        sometimes
a kind of light will spread across the sky and enter—can I say
        my heart?

And what it is is my happiness, a kind of flat buzz with a purity
        attached,
and since there's nothing new under the sun, what it is
is akin to the happiness of the one-dimensional characters
at the end of Hallmark specials, and who gives a fuck if that's a
        cliché—
who cares if it means that all I've done is just give up—
my happiness does whatever it wants and it's all I've ever
        wanted,
so what I am is ecstatic, waiting on the edge of my seat
for the angry boys to activate their spicy fires
and blow the lot of us (at long last) all up.

ÉTUDE FOR THE BIRTH YEAR

Always more and more writers writing more and more psalms.
Writers pulling on labia like origami in a row and sleeping with
        boas
and big, sundry fishes. Writers burning onions, licking seeds,
        smoking smokes,
drawing berries, snapping bras, fraying sweaters, aping owls,
and what I guess I meant before to say was *sobbing sobby sobs*

until what do I do
but notice my baby's upper lip like a figure in Matisse
lying on its side in a little dash of grass? Also her smell like tiny
        salt.
Her tongue on the nipple and her hair in the dark.
Because with a deft fury she beckons and giggles and weeps.

Because with ten fingers she reaches and with her nose then
        kisses.
Because from her own self she dribbles and listens and sings,
she like an onslaught rises to bury the drought:
she whom of love and spite and fear and sorrow
her young father and I last summer on the daybed made.

APRIL SONG FOR AUGUST

Since it's spring again, the sun is at it again:
stripping all over the place all over the park.
It has untapped the keg and unfurled the licorice
and the minstrels. It's unfurled the blush,
people. It's blown the safe and looted the loot.
As for the old troubles, they're just laundry—
neither comic nor pathetic, neither news nor not.
That he says and she says. That the dogs mire
and the wells bite. That the handsome adolescents,
whom we've assembled, as well, and love,
as well, curse and smolder, just like other folks.
That we ourselves, for some odd reason,
clot and age so methodically. As for my daughter,
she's water, it's my job to keep her from spilling
over or out while she waddles along beside me
like a wild duck or a daisy or a dance,
since she really is a whole silliness of girl-babble
and blithe and founding and fleece. O child,
O delirious impossibility—bridge, dream, howl,
hitch—please come hear this meager salute.

NAP TIME

This poem, which has just begun for you
but has been looming for years for me,
is trying to name the virtue of silence,
which is that there is a *bustle* inside it,
a ruckus of not-noise and not-people
I think you'd also hear
if you could just press your ear to the door
of the room inside which August is sleeping.
What I mean is the sound of her breathing
plus the clamor of figures moving around
inside her dreaming: me and Papa
at the park with her plus Weston and Ben
walking the streets in the thin, mid-winter,
post-school afternoon like unequaled bonus parents
who'll give her chocolate and say *Hush now,
don't tell Mom.* I mean also the sound
of something unknown moving the blinds
and baby-specific mumbles mingling and merging
like the molecules of water
when we draw her a bath and fill up the Sippie cup.
Over my head there are giant airplanes
flying to exotic places and inside these
people thinking *Come you coming season
and heal my soul-errored heart.*
If they were not up there and not going,
would they hear the hullabaloo

of the lights being out and the baby
being down? It's a minute reverberation
like a small boy blowing a low-key whistle
across the blue waters of a bay.
I mean, it's like electric medicine,
that white, white ricochet.

CHANNEL 58

...A world of made
is not a world of born—pity poor flesh

and trees, poor stars and stones, but never this
fine specimen of hypermagical

ultraomnipotence. We doctors know

a hopeless case if—listen: there's a hell
of a good universe next door, let's go

—e.e. cummings

DEMOCRACY AND ITS DISCONTENTS

She admits she's dumpy and unfashionable, uncertain about
      textiles, a run-of-the-mill concoction.
She admits she does not know how to whip or whisk the
      béarnaise sauce.
She admits she's proud, contrary, self-infected, insecure:
A wreck and a glutton in a corner of the riot at the edge of the
      world.
Thus sometimes to others she may seem distant, stuck-up,
      disruptive, a *blot*.
(Thus sometimes her obsession to prove she's got a working
      heart.)
For just one example, she loathes the Republicans.
She does not approve of their choice of car, by which she means
      the braggartness of it.
Ditto their choice of shirt—that button-up, dry-cleaned,
      labeled-on-the-outside white cotton blend.
Or so she thinks inside her hammerhead when she's strolling
      down the aisles in the grocery store
While touching her right breast to see how much milk there
      might be in it.
You can weigh that with your fingers. You can lift the breast and
      guess how much.
But who cares about breasts? Why even mention them?
All breasts are psychic scaffolding, or in this case the dastardly
      means by which

She might forestall admitting what she did that night her sister
    started yakking at the dinner table
About how she was going to put her kids in private school.
The sister said she didn't care for the grammatical errors of her
    less fortunate neighbors:
Those who lived on zip in trailers and those whose parents
    fumed on drink—
The odiferous shame of the backwardness of *those*.
At which point, as per the ancient family custom and to make a
    long story short,
She stood quite severely up to emphatically proclaim in her
    most haughty tone of voice
That it would be far more proper and in alightment with the
    original aims of America
For the sister to keep her kids in the public schools
And so sacrifice them in homage to the correct thinking of
    Thomas Jefferson.
Never you mind his incorrect thinking, for that was not her
    point.
There were also nineteen linen napkins.
There were red gladiolas in a crystal vase looking like blood
    blisters on stalks.
And yes she admits she felt like a reptile—abysmal, isolated,
    wet—the second the tirade began.
But do you understand that she nevertheless stood up and made
    her proclamation?

Oh, Thomas, what does it matter? When you said *the people*
    did you mean her, too,
Or was she shot out of the sky like some kind of sneering
    swallow
To sing the end of everything?

THE END OF BEAUTY

When I first began collecting my audience I knew nothing at all
and therefore had a lot of plans for the future of my audience.

I wanted my audience to sing and attempted consequently
to burn whale-air into their baby lungs because what I *really*
      wanted

was for my audience to embody me with poems manufactured I
      guess
from the history of blood and the annals of welts.

Ergo I prayed and partied; ergo I stood on the smoking block
and retreated after workshops to bars and lawns and lily-livered
      kitchens.

Because did I or did I *not* straddle the yellow ladder-backs?
Well, I was twenty-three. I lived in a small village

with my husband-the-photographer
and avoided sex by talking about it with my audience

and by being daring; I dared my audience to write what I dared
      not:
I dared it to speak the truth no matter how horrid.

Say murder! I said: *Truth is murder and murder, truth.*
In two weeks I'll insist on this statement even more
 emphatically

and my audience will write it down,
and in three weeks I'll say it again

and my audience will write it down, and always it will be me
dying before my audience like a common marigold at the end of
 September.

On this day all I want my audience to know
is that if the tone of this discourse seems unduly depressed—

if I sound here atypically despondent and despairing—
it's because all this time I've been after saying

what I didn't know as a young woman but do know now,
which is that none of us can be beautiful forever,

though we may dedicate ourselves to the tongue
and though the tongue may swell and the mouth open

and the news like the womb rent and rip.

FOR MY STUDENTS

Some of my students swallow Prozac and a fair number are
      lesbians.
Those who are not lesbians suffer the kind of sexual trouble
I relate to the housewives of the 1950's

and those who do not suffer that kind of trouble
stopped eating in the eighth grade
and walk around as if they're trying to become

contours or handmade walking canes.
If you say one word about peaches or peppergrass sauce—
peppergrass sauce is not a real food,

but one I just made up as I often do in class
to trick my students into trying to eat—
my students will bring in a teaspoon of yogurt, say,

and deposit it into their fiercely pink mouths
while simultaneously noting that the poem does bloom—
they'll say *bloom*—to its most ultimate point of grievance.

I know about my students' bodies
because my students write about their bodies.
I stay up late every single night

wondering if I should call my midwife to get the Blood Wort
and other herbal remedies. I mean, I worry constantly.
I mean, do Geometers worry constantly?

One day I'll leave this place
and my students will come back to me
like a million moths or stars or animal eyes.

I'll wake and walk to the nearest window
and look out on the air and imagine I smell some sorrows
in the winter wind, but it'll just be

my students out there making a go
of getting rid of me. I mean, it'll be this song.
I mean, already, already, already they're gone.

BAPTISM

Standing on a nickel, stripped of every single cloak:
stripped of mascara and of hot pants, stripped of the adolescent
       alibi;
stripped down to the grill, my hair stripped, my pout out;
stripped of the mother country and her farmhouses haunting
       the owls
ogling the blind barn bats; stripped of the boys calling out *Mama*

and the phone ringing it and the puny chicken
astringent in the oven and the bath fuming of me in Prell
and smoke and vodka; stripped of the ten thousand
       debaucheries:
of me thinking of fucking X and plotting extra ways I'd make
       him mine
and of missing Y and plotting the murder of Z, Y's ridiculous
       girlfriend

with her basement apartment and body arts and table crafts;
stripped of all the girls singing in the gym; stripped of girl-eye
and girl-ambition and girl-adoration; stripped of all my apt
       maidens
lined up in the hall with their bereavement notebooks
still battering against their ribs like ossified monkey bones,

I am stripped of my story, stripped from the crime scene
as though laid down in fishy river water
and brought up again to this still city night of chronic breathing,
this fastidious herb garden with its ignoble thyme blossoms
and pretty silver-green sage hedge blinking in barbarous calm.

CHANNEL 58

Now that I've got cable I can't think of anything else.
  Before cable I could avoid the glum idea
    of the end of the human heart

by cooking dinner in the kitchen
  while pretending I was Olivia from that show *The Waltons*.
    That was something I used to like to do.

Unlike Olivia, though, I'd always drink a little merlot in the
        kitchen
  and contemplate the 1960's
    and come to some all-purpose conclusions

about how free love was the most failed experiment
  of the so-called twentieth century.
    Like for instance that time

my mother and father and their small town tycoon friends
  Mr. and Mrs. Ralph Dollarpockets
    decided to have a nude dinner party

and Daddy and Diamond, being the artistic ones,
  danced naked to a little *Age of Aquarius*
    while Mama and Ralph, being much more no-nonsense,

discussed the real estate market on the couch
   drinking cocktails with their pinkies out.
      Later Diamond would leave Ralph and run off to Nashville

to try and become a famous country music star.
   I don't know if Diamond's famous or not,
      but probably she just got married to someone else

and bought another maybe even bigger house
   and had other dinner parties
      where people were obliged to wear their clothes.

No doubt Diamond has now a grandchild or two.
   My own mother does, if you want to know, and I guess
      I'll also be driving around with a grandchild in my van

before you know it, although right now
   I'm just on the verge of thirty-eight
      and it's a slow-burn Sunday afternoon

and I'm thinking about Britney Spears
   and the various rare and fatal diseases
      they present on the Health channel.

You might not know about the blood disease
   that turns a whole body to bone.
      You might not think such a thing's even possible,

but I saw the skeletons and some tow-headed four-year-olds
  being spoon-fed in special high chairs.
    Once you see such a thing, you can't think anymore

about the particulars of your ridiculous past.
  You obsess on Lot's wife instead
    and wonder if the bone disease is really what got her,

since even back then God may have been too busy
  watching the lesbians relate on Oxygen
    to muster up the rage to put an end to Sodom and
      Gomorrah.

Thinking about Sodom and Gomorrah
  does remind me of the 1960's,
    when people were just trying to get their sorry hearts
      together

or wake up somehow somehow somehow
    though from a certain child perspective (meaning mine)
    it looked like the drug overdose and psychedelic orgy

that it was. How so very heavy my students' eyelids get
  when I mention the 1960's and that search for the inner life.
    My students don't think much

about the inner life, but sometimes when I say they should
   they look down to their laps
      like they think it might be in their sexual organs.

I'd like to tell them that's where it is.
   I'd like to say the inner life can be relied upon
      to sound off like an alarm or ambulance

when you're just walking around the mall
   looking at photographs of the breasts of Britney Spears
      and wondering if they're fake or not.

But really the inner life isn't anywhere
   to speak of. You might find the inner life
      in a box of old birthday candles or in a drawer in the kitchen

while you're pretending to be the honorable Mrs. John Walton.
   Maybe the inner life is under the corkscrews and garlic presses
      or maybe beside some trees in the woods

where hippies maybe still meet and fuck and bellow,
   but ten to one it isn't and you'll just have to just go on buying
      whatever it is you buy

such as the coordinated outfits and the sex toys
   and the issue of *Teen People* magazine
      with the face of a certain star

staring out all wide-eyed and gorgeous
  like it was fine to walk around
    getting rich off your barren heart and your thumping groin,

which, since this is America, O my sleepy comrades, it is.

CASE AGAINST APRIL

For a long time I was absolutely idiotic,
by which I mean I lashed and pulsed
like the cosmos of tissue at present on fire
inside the bodies of my students—
it being springtime, it being the season
of being naked under the cherry trees.
I'm not saying dig a hole and fall in it;

I'm not saying buy a cabin and a nanny goat
and walk around re-naming the forget-me-nots
after the lovers who said they'd slay you
and, well, *did*—for who ever heard
of a plant named Greg? Nevertheless,
sex is laughable; it's ultimately ridiculous;
it's what God invented since he couldn't have

Comedy Central. And still the young people
who aren't pushing their tongues
against the tongues of others
are weeping like babies
being prodded with thermometers
for the lack of good tongues
to lean their own tongues against.

I hear them complaining
about their would-be boyfriends and girlfriends,
and it's like they are all about to die,
like their hearts have spontaneously combusted
and little cell splinters are poking their lungs
and they're losing their balance,
falling like hail

or like meteors with pretty faces,
which is why when I say *up,* they look down.
And though I'm all for biology,
for the divine plan of multiplication
that calls for the pink of bodies
being bodies with other bodies
in beds and in bushes,

I'm sorry for all the time I wasted
being dramatic over the boys and their mustaches.
Maybe the heart, it gets colder.
But maybe the heart,
it learns a little self-preservation
and pulls the shades down
one window at a time. And it's not dark

in here. Really, there's a kind of light
between the marrow and the bone,
and sweet patches of grass to lie down on,
and muskrats and pied pipers
if that's the way you like to see the world,
if to get your kicks you choose to be delirious.
I mean, if you happen to be romantic

and don't mind splitting apart with longing
like a child in a toy store
with everywhere these primary colors
seeming to want to open what could be mouths
and seeming to want to sing what could be songs
if only you could catch your breath—
if only your heart would just stop seizing.

INVECTIVE

Excuse me, but as to forgiving your aphid-headed enemies
because they must suffer atrocious childhoods and alchoholism

and a whole series of laughingstock love-annulments
and deficient genitalia and liability snags

like at-the-limit Visa cards and chipped coffee mugs
that whittle a little from the periphery of the lips

and fungal infections that wreck, I guess, the wits:
I just don't have it in me; I am not Jesus;

my father is an atheist and I was never baptized
and have anyhow spent my grownup years

watching kids bite each other on the arms and legs
while I thought my whiney thoughts about America-the-
      beautiful

with its Reality TV and McDonald's and Prozac and Liposuction
though soon everyone's going to have syphilis for starters

and there'll be a global shortage of Penicillin and a new Ice Age
and no heat no oil no fire at all but for the purblind, trampling,

aphid-headed among us whose wicked ways I will never pardon
because I guess I'm human: I think that's the problem:

I'm as infected as the snapdragons in my garden
with the rain-rot of being the person Adrian Blevins

and no I am not sorry, for it is the aphid-headed who should be
      sorry
though obviously they're not; they're just too nitwitted

and could furthermore use a few pointers
in what my Mama likes to call *the beauty department*.

WAKING UP

When the girl from the Exxon guns her engine with her derelict
        foot,
it's certain I am meant to awaken and listen to those suddenly-
        aroused
pipes and rings and filters. I always think she must want
        trouble.
Maybe I swiped her boyfriend in '78 when I was nothing but a
        carcass
and easy like all the shit from Elsewhere, but if I did, I'd like to
        say
I didn't mean it. Or maybe she just couldn't stand the blue
        dresses my mother sewed
that I couldn't stand, either. But probably it was something else,
a foul up with more death in it——something I said in third
        period English,
probably, some crazy thing I meant so much I'd have staked my
        life on it.
I don't remember being in high school, so I can't say if I
        offended the Exxon girl,
but I think she must live in a trailer. It must be horrible to work
        in a gas station,
and be over thirty, and I think there's a child, as sometimes she
        mentions one.
To tell her how sorry I am for whatever it is I did, I would like
        to nurse him,
as I would like to nurse all the children of America. Like the
        Exxon girl,

I don't remember getting married. I don't recall the day or how
    my husband looked
or who I was then when I was so blonde I was like the color of
    spring
bursting from the tips of winter. It does not please me to say
    how invisible I was
when I got married, but I was eighteen then and ignorant of
    everything
except for what would happen if I'd give myself over to a stupid
    boy's stupid cock.
When the boys would use their mammal parts against me
I'd appear in the world like magic ink coming up from the
    center of a page,
and when I found one who'd love me, though I couldn't see him
    and couldn't be seen—
oh, it was dismal there in the white space of being ignorant and
    eighteen,
and I was frightened, and didn't take to the world, so it must
    have been
as it often is in dreams—the way there's this vague shape
    moving around
that's got to be you, but you're on the outside, as if watching
    from the sun,
and when he moves in to kiss you, you just close your eyes
like you think you're Sleeping Beauty. And almost it's as if the
    whole kingdom

goes right down with you: each hydrant, each piece of board-
and-batten
in each house of every town and village, and it could go on for
hundreds of years—
the vines themselves asleep at the wheel—until some girl you
didn't even know
in high school presses a part of herself down real hard into the
flat, phallic gas pedal
of her automobile and you wake to find yourself alone in bed
with troubled, partly-grown boy-children sleeping right down
the hall.
That's when the world's so speechless you think you can hear
the dead
unbreathing in their graves. You think so much about the dead,
you think you know what it means to be in a body. That's what
rage is.
It's being too much inside yourself. It's waking up ten feet from
the Exxon
to a caterwauling motorcar. It's standing at the end of winter,
watching your sons sleep stony in the double bed while the
house loosens on its hinges
with such self-assurance, you know your babies will start
wailing any minute now.
And *that's* what waking is. It's wanting to be forgiven
for all the evil you can't remember doing, but know you must
have done.

NOTES & ACKNOWLEDGMENTS

Epigraphs:
Marilynne Robinson, *Housekeeping,* Noonday Press, 1980
Toni Cade Bambara, "The Johnson Girls," *Gorilla, My Love,*
    Random House, 1960
Marguerite Duras, *The Lover,* Pantheon, 1985
e.e. cummings, "pity this busy monster, manunkind," *Poems*
    1923–1954, Harcourt Brace Jovanovich, 1954
Stephanie Brown, "The Role of the Female Artist in Society,"
    Allegory of the Supermarket, University of Georgia Press,
    1999
John Berryman, "Of 1826," *The Dream Songs,* Farrar, Straus &
    Giroux, 1964

The first three lines of "The Other Cold War" constitute a slightly altered version of the opening sentences of J.D. Salinger's *The Catcher in the Rye,* Little Brown, 1945.

The quote in "Of Clichés and Superstitions" is from Eleanor Sinclair Rohde's *A Garden of Herbs,* Hale, Cushman & Flint, 1936.

I am grateful to the editors of magazines in which some of the poems in this manuscript first appeared, most in earlier versions.
A! Magazine for the Arts: "Nap Time"
Artemis: "Generally Speaking" (as "The Wilderness You Know Best")
Barkeater: The Adirondack Review: "Of Clichés and Superstitions"
The Drunken Boat: "Life History," "For My Students"
The Lucid Stone: "Hansel on the Highroad"

Nantahlaa: A Review of Writing and Photography in Appalachia: "The Magnificence of Rain," "Xanthe, The Master Gardner," "The Last Lap of the Daytona 500"

Ontario Review: "My Happiness," "Girl, 8th Grade," "November Neurosis"

Poet Lore: "Channel 58," "Women's Lib," "Case Against April"

Rivendell: "Democracy and its Discontents," "Kings of the Trampoline"

Southern Review: "Waking Up" (as "Waking"), "Turning 36"

I could express my gratitude to Tony Hoagland for his help with this book if I could plug it into a Marshall amp. But I have only these laughable sentences! Still, Tony, *thank you.* Thanks, too, to Steve Orlen and to my other Warren Wilson MFA Program friends— Robert, Patrick, Gary, and Amelia, just to name a few—for their encouragement and help. Finally, I am grateful to the students I taught at Hollins University from 1990–1999 for being among the best of my best teachers: the world would be too low and thin without you all in it.

I was able to revise this book in relative peace and quiet thanks to the generous financial assistance from The Rona Jaffe Writers' Foundation. Thanks to Rona, Beth, Bobbi, and all the other folks associated with the foundation for their support.

A few of the poems in this book first appeared, in earlier versions and some with different titles, in *The Man Who Went Out for Cigarettes*, a Bright Hill Press chapbook, Bright Hill Press, 1996, 1997.

CPSIA information can be obtained
at www.ICGtesting.com
Printed in the USA
LVOW07s0901310717
543241LV00003B/13/P